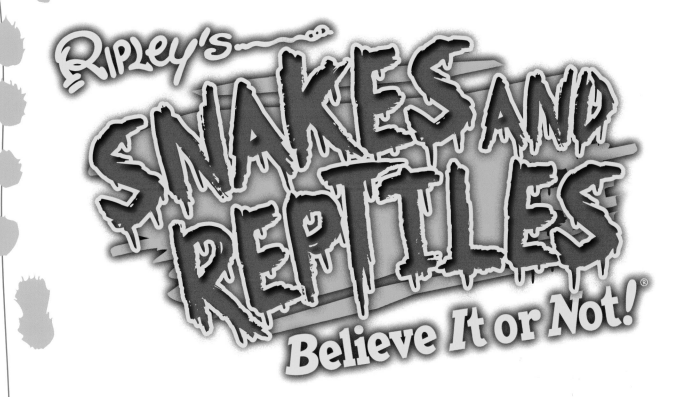

Ripley's SNAKES AND REPTILES

Believe It or Not!®

TWISTS

RIPLEY
PUBLISHING

a Jim Pattison Company

Written by Kezia Endsley
Cover Concept by Joshua Surprenant

RIPLEY PUBLISHING

Executive Vice President, Intellectual Property Norm Deska
Vice President, Archives and Exhibits Edward Meyer
Director, Publishing Operations Amanda Joiner
Managing Editor Dean Miller

Editor Jessica Firpi
Designer Michelle Foster
Researcher Sabrina Sieck
Additional Research Jessica Firpi
Fact Checker James Proud
Production Coordinator Amy Webb
Reprographics Juice Creative Ltd

www.ripleys.com/books

Published by Ripley Publishing 2015

Ripley Publishing 7576 Kingspointe Parkway, Suite 188
Orlando, Florida 32819 USA

10 9 8 7 6 5 4 3 2 1

Copyright © 2015 by Ripley Entertainment Inc.

ISBN 978-1-60991-141-6

Library of Congress Control Number: 2015942039

Manufactured in China in June 2015.
First Printing

PAGE 37

CONTENTS

TWISTS

PAGE 19

PAGE 10

WILD WORLD

MARVELOUS CREATURES

WHAT'S INSIDE YOUR BOOK?

Green tree boas from the Amazon River Basin grow 7 to 10 feet long in length.

Emerald green tree boas have been known to grab birds that are in mid-flight.

If you just take a minute to pause, you'll find exceptional reptiles flourishing all around, even in your own backyard. But how much do you really know about them?

Join us on a trip around the world, where you'll discover the kingdom of the reptiles, cold-blooded creatures that cover the planet and have been thriving on Earth since the time of the dinosaurs. Reptiles have a diverse and adaptable way of life, and you won't believe the extremes they endure to survive and thrive!

TWISTS

These books are about "Believe It or Not!"— amazing facts, feats, and things that make you go "Wow!"

Ripley's Believe It or Not!

Zoologists at the University of Florida operated on a pine snake that had swallowed two light bulbs! Doctors were successful in removing the bulbs, and the snake actually survived to be re-released into the wild!

Found a new word? Big word alerts will explain it for you.

BIG WORD ALERT

CLUTCH

A group of eggs hatched at the same time.

Look out for the "Twist It" column on some pages. Twist the book to find out more amazing facts about snakes and other reptiles!

AAHH! THEY ARE EVERYWHERE!

REPTILES RULE THE ROOST

Reptiles make their homes in so many amazing places. Check out their exotic habitats across the world!

Reptiles live on every continent except Antarctica. Reptiles are found in deserts, rain forests, wooded forests, lakes, rivers, salty oceans, and even underground!

TWIST IT!

In 1968, the Soviet Union launched the Zond 5 spacecraft carrying a pair of tortoises that became the first animals to ever enter deep space!

A runway at John F. Kennedy International Airport in New York City was shut down briefly in 2009 after about 80 turtles crawled onto the tarmac!

Most reptiles can't tolerate the cold, but the Blanding's turtle is sometimes found swimming under the ice in the Great Lakes region of the United States!

Small garter snakes can live in parts of northern Canada, where it's so cold that the snakes hibernate for eight months of the year!

The web-footed gecko lives in the African desert and drinks dew from its eyeballs every morning to keep cool and hydrated.

SCALY SKIN

WHITE-LIPPED PIT VIPER

Snakes live everywhere but Ireland, New Zealand, and the North and South Poles. These bright green pit vipers live in tropical forests and scrublands all throughout Asia.

FACINATING FACTS

You're in lizard territory.

The bigger the lizard, the bigger its territory. Small lizards might have a territory no bigger than your bedroom, whereas the Komodo dragon, which can grow as big as 10 feet long, might roam a much larger territory. Territory size also depends on food availability—the more scarce food is, the larger a lizard's territory must be.

BLUNT-NOSED LEOPARD LIZARD

Desert reptiles use the morning sun to warm up after a cold desert night but then spend the rest of the day hiding in burrows and under rocks to avoid the scorching daylight.

PANTHER CHAMELEON

The island of Madagascar is home to these beautiful chameleons made up of 11 different species! The color patterns of panther chameleons depend on their geographical location, and the males usually have more vibrant colors.

EASTERN COLLARED LIZARD

Ripley Explains...

See the "Ripley explains" panels for extra info from our snakes and reptiles experts.

Turn over to find out more about snakes and reptiles.

REPTILES

THE REAL DEAL

Scaly but not slimy, and only sometimes venomous!

Most reptiles are harmless and shy, but they still freak some people out. Oddly enough, they aren't slimy, don't want to hurt you, and are incredible relics from an ancient time!

Living on Earth at least 300 million years, reptiles include snakes, crocodiles and alligators, lizards, and turtles and tortoises. They are ectotherms, meaning they must use the air temperature to stay comfortable—not too hot nor too cold.

Sturdy Sea Turtle

Reptiles lay their watertight, leathery eggs on land. This sea turtle has to work hard to break free from her egg's sturdy shell.

Did you know that there are over 9,000 types of reptiles on Earth?

Hairy Bush Viper

Reptile scales are dry and watertight. They come in a variety of colors, and some can even change color depending on their mood and environment.

Reptiles are extremely versatile and can live in many different types of climates.

TWIST IT!

More Americans die each year from wasp and bee stings than from snake bites.

In 1987, the American alligator became Florida's official state reptile.

February 1 is National Serpent Day!

In Illinois, there is a law requiring any person selling a reptile to give written notice to the buyer stating, "Don't nuzzle or kiss your pet reptile."

SCALY SCOOP

Research shows that humans can detect images of snakes more quickly among other non-threatening images, furthering the idea that humans have developed the ability to sense snakes and fear them.

Reptiles need the sun's heat to survive, so they are most common in hotter areas.

Marine Lizards
Marine iguanas are found exclusively in the Galápagos Islands and are the world's only seafaring lizards!

LEGS, SCALES, AND SHELLS, OH MY!

Reptiles are an ancient group of animals sharing common characteristics. Although they share ancestors and millions of years of evolution, they differ in many ways from each other.

Reptiles have dry, waterproof skin, and all reptile skin is covered in scales (made from keratin) that vary in form depending on the animal.

DISGUSTING OR DELIGHTFUL?

You decide...

Fierce and powerful, crocodiles and alligators have horny scales and hard plates that cover their bodies.

This snake was discovered in China in 2009 with a rare mutation: a single clawed foot growing out from its body. The 16-in-long mutant reptile was found by Duan Qiongxiu clinging to the wall of her bedroom with its talons. Terrified, Mrs. Duan killed the snake with her shoe.

Thorny Devil Defense

The scales of a thorny devil lizard consist of hard sharp spines, making it hard to swallow.

Ripley Explains...

Evolved from legged lizards, legless lizards are not snakes at all. Similar to snakes in behavior and appearance, legless lizards have fixed jaws, moveable eyelids, ear openings, and the ability to detach their tail in an emergency.

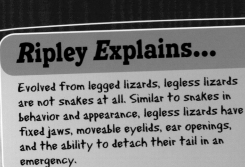

BIG WORD ALERT
KERATIN

Reptile scales, like our hair and fingernails, are made of keratin (a fibrous protein).

TURTLE SHELL SHOCK

Turtles and tortoises carry their homes around on their backs. A turtle's shell is covered in scales called scutes, which strengthen the shell bone.

Well, what do you think—are reptiles terrific or terrible?

Eye Lash Viper

Snakes have no legs and have scales of various shapes and sizes. Some scales have been modified over time, such as the rattle on rattlesnakes or the "eye lashes" on certain snakes.

WHAT'S IN A SHAPE?

Reptiles have evolved fantastic shapes, body parts, and defenses to help ensure their survival.

Some reptiles have shells, fangs, or even color-changing scales to help protect them from predators. However, for other reptiles, it's what they DON'T have (like eyelids, ears, or even legs) that helps keep them safe. When it comes to survival of the fittest, reptiles have almost every angle covered!

FUNCTIONAL AND
FANTASTIC FORMS

Located in the middle of Kakadu National Park in Australia, the Gagudju Crocodile Holiday Inn is shaped to look just like the saltwater crocodile, which is native to the region!

Fierce Front

When threatened, cobras spread out their neck ribs to form a flattened, widened hood around their head.

TWIST IT!

A blindworm is neither blind nor a worm—it is actually a legless lizard!

Egg-eating snakes have sharp spines along their backbones that extend into the esophagus and break the eggshell. The snake regurgitates the crushed shell after swallowing the egg's contents.

Baby rattlesnakes are born without rattles!

Alligators and crocodiles have flaps of skin that seal their ears, nose, and throat from water, while a double pair of eyelids protects their eyes.

SHAPE CENTRAL

Supple Skin

Instead of having horny scutes (scales) on their shells, softshell turtles simply have thickened skin. Their light and flexible shells allow for easier movement in open water or muddy lake bottoms as well as faster movement on land.

Master of Disguise

The satanic leaf-tailed gecko from Madagascar takes camouflage to the extreme! It can change colors—including purple, orange, tan, yellow, brown, and black— blending perfectly into their forest habitat.

When faced with predators, bearded lizards flare out their throats to look intimidating.

AHH! THEY ARE EVERYWHERE!

REPTILES RULE THE ROOST

Reptiles make their homes in so many amazing places. Check out their exotic habitats across the world!

Reptiles live on every continent except Antarctica. Reptiles are found in deserts, rain forests, wooded forests, lakes, rivers, salty oceans, and even underground!

PANTHER CHAMELEON

The island of Madagascar is home to these beautiful chameleons made up of 11 different species! The color patterns of panther chameleons depend on their geographical location, and the males usually have more vibrant colors.

TWIST IT!

In 1968, the Soviet Union launched the Zond 5 spacecraft carrying a pair of tortoises that became the first animals to ever enter deep space!

A runway at John F. Kennedy International Airport in New York City was shut down briefly in 2009 after about 80 turtles crawled onto the tarmac!

Most reptiles can't tolerate the cold, but the Blanding's turtle is sometimes found swimming under the ice in the Great Lakes region of the United States!

Small garter snakes can live in parts of northern Canada, where it's so cold that the snakes hibernate for eight months of the year!

The web-footed gecko lives in the African desert and drinks dew from its eyeballs every morning to keep cool and hydrated.

WHITE-LIPPED PIT VIPER

Snakes live everywhere but Ireland, New Zealand, and the North and South Poles. These bright green pit vipers live in tropical forests and scrublands all throughout Asia.

SCALY SKIN

BLUNT-NOSED
LEOPARD LIZARD

FACINATING FACTS
You're in lizard territory.

The bigger the lizard, the bigger its territory. Small lizards might have a territory no bigger than your bedroom, whereas the Komodo dragon, which can grow as big as 10 feet long, might roam a much larger territory. Territory size also depends on food availability—the more scarce food is, the larger a lizard's territory must be.

Desert reptiles use the morning sun to warm up after a cold desert night but then spend the rest of the day hiding in burrows and under rocks to avoid the scorching daylight.

EASTERN
COLLARED LIZARD

WHAT'S FOR DINNER?

THE MEALTIME MENU

Most lizards and snakes are carnivores and snack on small animals, insects, birds, and even other reptiles. Only a small handful, like very large iguanas, are herbivores and eat only plants.

From sticky tongues and venomous bites, to hiding in plain sight for a surprise attack, reptiles have special ways of hunting for a meal. Reptiles also use camouflage to hunt, not just to hide from predators.

Some chameleons have tongues longer than their bodies!

Ripley's Believe It or Not!

Reggie, a 3-ft-long kingsnake, swallowed his own tail after he mistook it for another snake and was unable to regurgitate it because of his rear-facing teeth. Luckily, a veterinary surgeon removed the tail before it had been digested.

BIG WORD ALERT

CARNIVORE

An animal whose diet consists mainly of meat.

HERBIVORE

An animal whose diet consists mainly of plants.

Snakes can swallow animals larger than their head with their flexible jaws.

TWIST IT!

In 2011, on the Greek island of Corfu, a lucky Dahl's whip snake wriggled its way to freedom after being eaten by a four-lined snake, which was in turn killed by a pet cat!

Temperature affects how fast a meal is digested—the warmer the snake, the faster the digestion.

The Subtropical Teahouse is a "reptile café" in Japan where customers can observe and pet dozens of species.

The smallest of all snakes, the Barbados thread snake, is so small it can only eat the pupae (or eggs) of insects like ants, termites, and centipedes.

READY REPTILES

Ripley Explains... Chomp Chomp

Alligator Snapping Turtle

The alligator snapping turtle rests on the riverbed with its mouth open to trick fish into coming near to eat the "worm"—a bright-red, worm-shaped piece of flesh on its tongue. When the fish try to attack the worm, the turtle clamps its jaws shut and enjoys its meal.

VS.

Alligators and Crocodiles

Alligators and crocodiles hide in the water and ambush other animals coming for a drink. Although almost completely under water, they can still hear, see, and breathe. They eat fish, rabbits, turtles, snakes, and even large mammals like deer and buffalo!

FANGS AND JAWS GALORE!

ARMED TO THE TEETH!

From bites and venom to spikes and poison, the fangs and jaws of certain reptiles should not be underestimated!

When hiding or running doesn't work, reptiles might just strike back! Only after giving plenty of warnings will they attack in self-defense. Of course, reptiles use their powerful jaws and fangs to attack and devour their dinner.

KOMODO KILLER!

The Komodo dragon, found only on a few Indonesian islands, is the biggest lizard on Earth and is extremely venomous. The venom ducts in its lower jaw release venom into the blood that hastens death by decreasing blood pressure, sending the victim into shock.

MONSTER MOUTHFUL!

The Indian Gharial crocodile has an extra long snout with over 100 razor-sharp teeth that developed so they can catch and eat small fish easily.

Although most snakes have teeth, not all snakes have fangs—only the venomous ones do.

ATROCIOUS CHOPS!

Boa constrictor jaws are lined with small, hooked teeth for grabbing and holding prey, which helps as they squeeze their victims.

DEFENSE: THE BEST OFFENSE

FIGHTING FOR SURVIVAL

Reptiles live in a dangerous world where many animals would love to have them for lunch—they are both predators and prey. Reptiles have various ways to protect themselves against attack.

Some reptiles use camouflage to hide, whereas others confuse or fool attackers by using clever tricks: looking bigger than they really are, dropping their tails when attacked, and using warnings like rattles or blood to caution predators. Other reptiles have thorns and shells to protect themselves.

When under attack, many lizards can detach their tails and escape. Their tails will grow back without much harm to the lizard.

Armadillo Lizard

Armadillo lizards are so named because of the armadillo-like tactic they use to avoid predators. When in danger, armadillo lizards curl into a ball that is inedible for most animals because of the spines on the neck and tail.

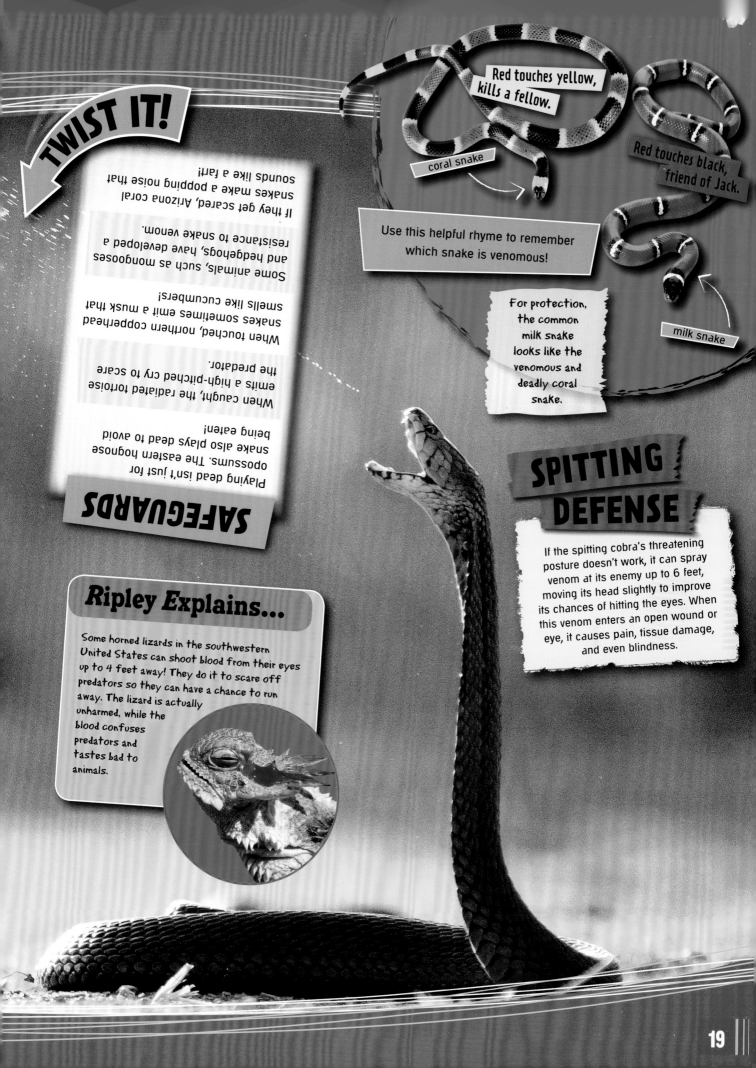

TWIST IT!

If they get scared, Arizona coral snakes make a popping noise that sounds like a fart!

Some animals, such as mongooses and hedgehogs, have developed a resistance to snake venom.

When touched, northern copperhead snakes sometimes emit a musk that smells like cucumbers!

When caught, the radiated tortoise emits a high-pitched cry to scare the predator.

SAFEGUARDS

Playing dead isn't just for opossums. The eastern hognose snake also plays dead to avoid being eaten!

Ripley Explains...

Some horned lizards in the southwestern United States can shoot blood from their eyes up to 4 feet away! They do it to scare off predators so they can have a chance to run away. The lizard is actually unharmed, while the blood confuses predators and tastes bad to animals.

Red touches yellow, kills a fellow.

coral snake

Red touches black, friend of Jack.

Use this helpful rhyme to remember which snake is venomous!

milk snake

For protection, the common milk snake looks like the venomous and deadly coral snake.

SPITTING DEFENSE

If the spitting cobra's threatening posture doesn't work, it can spray venom at its enemy up to 6 feet, moving its head slightly to improve its chances of hitting the eyes. When this venom enters an open wound or eye, it causes pain, tissue damage, and even blindness.

EGGS-ACTLY!

LAYING EGGS IS THEIR BUSINESS!

Nearly all reptiles lay eggs, but the process and results differ greatly depending on the animal.

Most reptiles are born on land, not in water. They lay their eggs in underground burrows, which keeps the eggs warm and protects them from other animals. Reptiles that have fewer young at a time and give birth to live babies are usually more caring and supportive parents.

Greater short-horned lizards are one of the few lizards that give birth to live babies and care for their young after birth. It carries its babies on its back to keep them safe.

Unlike many reptiles, alligators and crocodiles nurture their young for up to a year, carrying them around in their mouths and keeping them safe from predators.

Laying their eggs in one basket?

* Tortoises and crocodiles lay eggs with hard shells, whereas most turtles, lizards, and snakes lay eggs with soft, leathery shells (although some turtles do lay hard shells).

* Developing reptile babies get their food from inside the wet, yolky egg. The outer layer of the egg keeps it from drying out on land.

* Some snakes (e.g., adders) and lizards (e.g., blue-tongued skinks) give birth to live young. Reptile babies that hatch inside the mother usually have a better chance of surviving.

THE BIG HATCH

To lay their eggs, female sea turtles swim as far as 1,000 miles or more back to the same beach where they were born.

Collecting leaves, sticks, and other vegetation, the King Cobra is the only snake in the world that builds a nest like a bird!

Reptile babies have a special "egg" tooth that they use to break open their shell at the time of birth.

Egg-eating snakes do not lay their own eggs all in one place—instead, they scatter the eggs in multiple locations.

The smallest known snake, the Barbados thread snake, is so small it can only lay one egg at a time.

TWIST IT!

For many reptiles, the temperature of the nest determines the gender of the baby.

21

FANG-TASTIC!

VENOMOUS SNAKES

Like all animals, snakes face danger when they are hunting for food. Their prey doesn't want to be eaten and will fight back to survive! Venomous snakes have a natural advantage that makes them more successful hunters.

Venomous snakes inject their prey using fangs—special sharp hollow teeth—that poke holes in the victim before the venom flows into the body, overpowering the prey so the snake can safely eat.

Ways to tell if a snake might be venomous:

* Shape of its head. If the head is triangular or heart shaped, stay away!

* Eye/pupil shape. When the pupil is a slit, instead of round, back off!

BOOMSLANG

Boomslangs are rear-fanged snakes. The fangs near the back of their mouths allow the venom to seep into the bite wounds.

sea snakes

Sea snakes are some of the most venomous of all snakes, but they don't bite humans very often, since humans are not their prey.

SNAKE BITE

Snakes retain biting reflexes for some time after death. A chef in China preparing cobra soup, a rare delicacy, was fatally bitten by the decapitated head of the meal's main ingredient!

Some snakes, like the *Rhabdophis tigrinus*, can actually steal poison from their prey, collecting it in glands to use for defense.

In the town of Ban Kok Sa-Nga (aka Cobra Village) in Thailand's northeast province, nearly every home has a pet snake.

A new snake species found in Panama in 2013 was named Sibon noalamina, or "No to the mine" in English, because its habitat is under threat from mining.

There are some 50 different species of sea snakes, and all of them are venomous.

TWIST IT!

Venomous snake fangs allow the venom to flow from the gland behind the fangs into the victim, like a needle.

Ripley Explains...

How does venom work?

Different types of chemicals called "toxins" exist in snake venom. The purpose of the toxin is to conquer or kill the victim, which can be done in different ways:

* Some toxins attack the blood or muscles, possibly paralyzing the animal or causing internal bleeding.

* Some toxins attack the nervous system so the victim suffocates.

* Some toxins attack the heart muscles causing direct damage to the heart.

Toxins flow quickly through the blood so their effects are felt instantly. Scientists have created antivenoms that reduce the effects of snakebites, and they work well if the victim is treated quickly.

MODERN ARCHOSAURS

ALL ABOUT CROCS AND GATORS

With ancestors living alongside dinosaurs, crocodiles and alligators are directly related to a group of extinct creatures called Archosaurs. Today's crocodiles and alligators are more closely related to birds than to other reptiles.

Crocs and gators belong to the *Crocodilian* group of reptiles and are the world's largest (but not the longest) reptiles. With powerful jaws and tails, they take down and feast on animals as large as deer and buffalo! Although fierce meat-eating predators, they are also very attentive parents and live in social packs.

Crocodiles and alligators have over 70 sharp, pointy teeth. When they lose teeth, new ones grow in.

Chinese alligator

There are only two types of alligators: the American Alligator, which resides in the southeastern United States, and the Chinese alligator, which is now very rare.

Close Cousins

What's the difference between crocs and gators?

Crocodiles...

* have a longer, narrower, more v-shaped snout
* live in the wild all over the world
* can live in freshwater and salty oceans
* generally have lighter-colored scales
* are more aggressive
* have visible upper and lower teeth when their mouth is closed

Alligators...

* have a wider, more u-shaped snout
* live only in the United States and China
* live in freshwater
* generally have darker-colored scales
* are less aggressive
* have hidden lower teeth but visible upper teeth when their mouth is closed

TWIST IT!

BIG BRUTES

When alligators close their mouths, every fourth tooth fits into a socket in the top jaw.

Crocodiles release heat through their mouths rather than through sweat glands, which is why they sunbathe with their mouths open.

Palaeontologists discovered ancient, dinosaur-eating crocodiles galloping, in the Sahara Desert of Africa.

A crocodile in a Ukrainian park accidentally ate a cell phone dropped by a visitor—and it continued to ring inside the animal's stomach!

Saltwater crocs, the largest Crocodilian group, can grow to over 23 feet long. That's as long as about four grown men lying head to toe!

LIVING FOSSILS

ALL ABOUT TURTLES AND TORTOISES

Turtles and tortoises have been on Earth since the time of the dinosaurs. They have changed very little since those ancient times—other than generally getting smaller—thus many people call them "living fossils." There are more than 250 different species living on Earth today.

They are the only *vertebrates* (animals with backbones) with hard shells. Covered with scaly plates called scutes, their shells grow and expand as they age, and the animals can never leave their shells. When threatened, many species pull their heads and legs completely into their shell for protection.

KEY FACTS

* All turtles and tortoises lay their eggs on land, which is the only time sea turtles leave their ocean home.

* The first turtles lived on Earth about 200 million years ago.

* Tortoises use their strong front limbs to dig burrows.

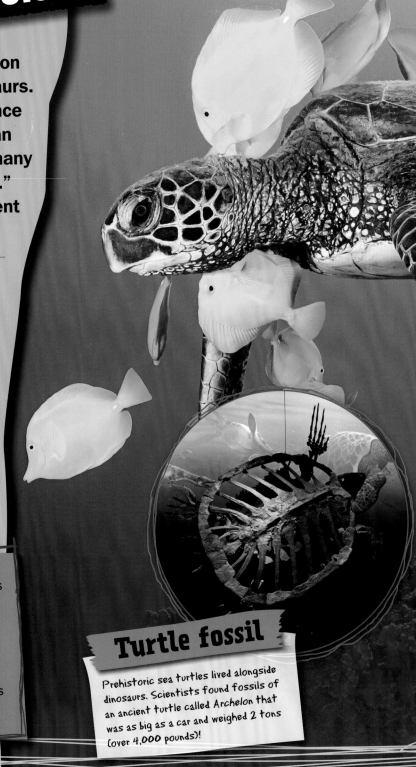

Turtle fossil

Prehistoric sea turtles lived alongside dinosaurs. Scientists found fossils of an ancient turtle called Archelon that was as big as a car and weighed 2 tons (over 4,000 pounds)!

Brothers in Armor

What's the difference between turtles and tortoises?

Turtles...

* live mostly in water (and at times on land)

* are found in every ocean except for the Arctic

* have flippers, webbed feet, and streamlined bodies for swimming

* eat fish and other marine creatures

Tortoises...

* live on land, usually in hot, dry places

* are native to every continent except Australia and Antarctica

* have round, stumpy feet for walking on sand, gravel, and dirt

* eat low-growing shrubs, grasses, fruits, vegetables, and flowers

TWIST IT!

TURTLE TIME

Turtles and tortoises can hibernate during the cold winter months by burying themselves in mud and living off their body fat. They might not move for two to three months!

Terrapins are a kind of hybrid between turtles and tortoises. Like their amphibian cousins, terrapins spend equal amounts of time in the water and on land and are always found near water.

May 23 is World Turtle Day. An international team of scientists have successfully trained four red-footed tortoises to use a touchscreen computer.

BIG WORD ALERT

CARAPACE
The top part of a turtle's shell.

PLASTRON
The bottom part of a turtle's shell.

sea turtle

Unlike land-bound turtles, sea turtles have flatter, more flexible carapaces and plastrons and flipper-like feet for navigating the oceans. Since they cannot pull their bodies into their shells, they must swim away quickly to avoid predators.

Galápagos tortoise

The Galápagos giant tortoise is the largest living species of tortoise and one of the heaviest living reptiles. They are found in the wild on a few Pacific Ocean islands, can weigh over 500 pounds, and live for more than 100 years.

LEGLESS LURKERS

ALL ABOUT SNAKES!

Snakes evolved from lizards, and some snakes, such as pythons and boas, still have tiny traces of back legs. However, they are not simply "legless lizards"—snakes are different in many ways.

Snakes are adaptable, living in trees, deserts, lakes and oceans, and even underground. They are dedicated hunters, yet only a small percentage of snakes are venomous. They differ from other reptiles in that they don't have ears or eyelids. Instead, snakes have other sophisticated ways of finding food and sensing danger.

snake jawbone

The snake's lower jaw is hinged to its skull, which allows it to open its mouth incredibly wide. This is important since all snakes swallow their prey whole.

Snakes use their forked tongues to "smell" and "taste" what is near them, which is why they often flick their tongues in and out.

KEY FACTS

* Snakes don't have eyelids and therefore never blink. Instead, they have a moist, clear scale that protects their eyes and sheds with the rest of their skin.

* Snakes don't have ears—instead, their jawbones are linked to sensors that sense vibrations on the ground.

* Some snakes have a hole at the bottom of their mouths called the glottis that allows them to breathe even when their mouth is chock-full of prey!

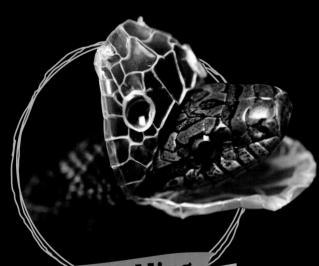

Snake shedding

When a snake outgrows its skin, the inner skin layer makes an oily fluid that removes the outer layer, allowing the snake to slip it off in one piece.

Leg spurs

Boas and pythons have "leg spurs," which are likely left over from their lizard ancestors. This tiny bit of leftover leg is called a vestigial limb.

Beating odds of more than 10,000 to one, a two-headed albino Honduran milk snake was hatched by a Florida conservation group. A few days later, the snake's right head ate its first meal while the left head watched.

TWIST IT!

Burmese pythons enlarge their own hearts by up to 40% when eating!

The largest snake fossil species ever discovered is called Titanoboa; a monster 50-ft-long snake that lived 60 million years ago.

Many snakes hibernate together in clusters in underground caves during the cooler months. This is one way that snakes living in colder habitats stay warm and survive.

The word cobra comes from the Portuguese cobra de capello, which means "snake with a hood."

Venomous snakes can accidentally bite themselves and die from their own venom! It's not common, but it can happen when snakes are under a lot of stress.

FORKED TONGUES

Pit viper

Pit vipers have special pits (holes) under their eyes that contain infrared heat sensors that allow them to "see" warm-blooded prey (such as mice) in total darkness!

BIG WORD ALERT

GLOTTIS

The hole at the bottom of a snake's mouth that allows it to breathe even when its mouth is chock full of prey.

MOVERS AND SHAKERS

MOVING WITHOUT LEGS!

Snakes move quickly and in ways that other animals cannot. Because they have strong muscles and hundreds of bones in their spines, they can move sideways and vertically, creep along in an "s" movement, burrow and climb, quickly strike, swim, and stand tall—all without feet!

Snakes can bend and coil their bodies to move quickly across loose or hot surfaces. Traveling in wavelike movements called undulations, they use their muscles to push off from the ground and other obstacles in their path. Snakes also move by gripping the ground with the curves of their bodies and then stretching out.

Snake skeleton

Snakes can bend in several directions at once, and their long backbones are the key to their movement.

Some snakes have more than 400 bones in their bodies and tails!

Sea snakes are the best swimmers because their tails are flattened like a paddle. They can dive deep and stay underwater for over an hour!

Snake swimming

All snakes are good swimmers. They use the serpentine method to move through the water, which works well because water is dense and gives snakes something strong

VERTEBRA

A fancy word for a small bone in the back. We have about 30 of them, and snakes have them too.

The more vertebrae an animal has, the more agile and flexible it is!

Ripley's Believe It or Not!®

Researchers have successfully created various snake robots, or "snakebots"! These snakebots can climb, crawl, and even scale trees. Snakebots can one day be used in search-and-rescue missions and possibly help NASA explore other worlds, like Mars!

Flying snake

As seen in this multiple exposure image, some Southeast Asian snakes even seem to fly! They hide high up in trees, and when they see prey such as lizards, they launch themselves into the air, flattening their bodies into the long ribbon. The air and wind under its ribbon-shaped body keep it afloat, and it uses its tail to steer.

Ripley Explains...

Snake Movement

Snakes have four main ways of moving:

Concertina Gripping the ground with the front half of their body, they pull their tail forward, creating an "s" shape.

Serpentine Snakes use their muscles to push against obstacles. As they wriggle, waves pass down their bodies from head to tail.

Sidewinding Sidewinders "throw" the front part of their body sideways, and a wave passing along its body enables the back to follow the front.

...raise their bodies off the ground, head first, and ...in the ground.

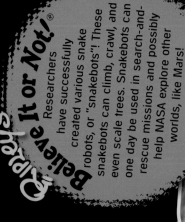

REMARKABLE REPTILES

ALL ABOUT LIZARDS

Lizards are the most common and numerous reptile on the planet. Scientists have found almost 6,000 species of lizards—more than all other reptiles combined!

Most lizards are carnivores and eat insects, spiders, scorpions, centipedes, and even other lizards. Larger lizards (like iguanas) are sometimes herbivores, eating flowers, fruits, and leaves. Since lizards are typically hunted and eaten by other animals, many use camouflage to hide.

ACTUAL SIZE

1 inch long!

Tiny Lizard

Lizards vary greatly in size. This tiny dwarf leaf chameleon is about an inch long.

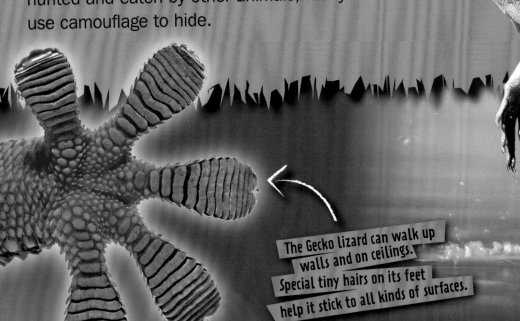

The Gecko lizard can walk up walls and on ceilings. Special tiny hairs on its feet help it stick to all kinds of surfaces.

LIZARD LUCK

An iguana can stay under water comfortably for up to 30 minutes.

A protein in the western fence lizard's blood can kill the bacterium that causes Lyme disease (fever, headache, skin rash), fatigue, and a "bull's-eye" skin rash) feed on the lizard's blood, the ticks leave so when disease-carrying ticks feed no longer carrying the disease!

The tuatara lizard of New Zealand has three eyes—two on either side of its head and one on top.

Flying lizard

Draco lizards are able to glide through the air because of skin flaps that spread out from their ribs to catch the air while the smaller neck flaps help them steer.

Basilisk lizards

("Jesus Christ" lizard)

Green basilisk lizards can run across the surface of water to catch insects. They do this thanks to their long toes with fringes of skin that unfurl in the water. By quickly slapping their feet hard against the water, they can travel across the water's surface at up to 5 feet per second.

Ripley Explains...

How can they change color like that?

Lizard skin is covered with layers of special cells called chromatophores. These cells contain tiny sacs of color and respond to chemicals that the lizard releases. They have only four colors to work with (yellow, red, blue, and brown) but they can mix colors (like mixing red and yellow to produce orange).

A lizard's own paint by numbers set!

Ripley's **Believe It or Not!**®
Photographer Aditya Permana captured this once-in-a-lifetime photo of a forest dragon lizard lazily playing a leaf guitar in Yogyakarta, Indonesia.

Many lizards live in underground burrows. These burrows are used for shelter from predators and midday desert heat.

CHARMING CHAMPS

ALL CREATURES, GREAT AND SMALL

Sporting some impressive members, the reptile family comes in all shapes and sizes. Find out how the biggest and the smallest contenders stack up against each other!

LIZARDS

CROCODILIAN

1ST

For the largest overall size and weight, the winner is the saltwater crocodile.

LARGEST

Giant Saltwater Croc

These crocs live near the salty shores surrounding much of Australia and the Indian Ocean and are known to occasionally eat humans, so watch out!

SIZE: Can grow to over 23 ft long

WEIGHT: Over 2,200 lbs

Cuvier's Dwarf Caiman

SMALLEST

Found in northern and central South America, dwarf caiman live alone or in pairs and eat fish, crab, mollusks, shrimp, and terrestrial invertebrates.

SIZE: Typically 4–5 ft long

WEIGHT: 13–15 lbs

Komodo Dragon

The name comes from rumors that a dragon-like creature lived on the Indonesian island of Komodo. Komodo dragons are fierce hunters and eat large prey, like water buffalo, deer, carrion, pigs, other smaller dragons, and even humans!

SIZE: Up to 10 ft long

WEIGHT: Up to 366 lbs

Leatherback Sea Turtle

Leatherbacks can dive to depths of 4,200 feet—deeper than any other turtle—and can stay down for up to 85 minutes. Leatherbacks are also able to maintain warm body temperatures in cold water by using a unique set of adaptations, so they have the widest global distribution of all reptile species.

SIZE: Up to 7 ft long
WEIGHT: Up to 2,000 lbs

LARGEST

The Komodo dragon is the largest lizard in the world!

LARGEST

This dwarf gecko is about the size of a dime!

SMALLEST

SMALLEST

Dwarf Geckos

There are several tiny lizards and geckos fighting for smallest reptile, but the Jaragua Sphaero (*Sphaerodactylus ariasae*) dwarf gecko is the tiniest! It lives on the remote Caribbean island of Beata, part of the Dominican Republic.

SIZE: 0.63–0.71 in long

Speckled Tortoise

Found in South Africa, their speckles help to keep them camouflaged in rocky areas, where they spend a great deal of their time hiding.

SIZE: 2.4–3.9 in long

RADICAL REPTILES

Reptiles often develop extreme traits because these traits help them survive in a very specific habitat. These traits might seem "extreme" to us, but they provide reptiles with their best chances for survival and reproduction.

FRILLED LIZARD

When faced with predators, frilled lizards flare out their neck frills in an intimidating threat display.

Whether it's all about the looks or more about function, these reptiles are really radical!

MATA MATA TURTLE

Called by many "the weirdest-looking turtle ever," this Amazonian turtle has a very long, snake-like neck and an odd mouth filled with two sharp plates resembling human teeth that are stuck together. It eats fish, water birds, and other reptiles.

SPIDER-TAILED HORNED VIPER

The spider-tailed horned viper uses its unique tail as a lure, shaking and wiggling it to mimic the movement of a spider. When birds approach and peck the tail, the snake makes its lightning-fast move.

TWIST IT!

Adwaita, an Aldabra Giant Tortoise from India, lived to be about 255 years old—which means he was born around 1750. That made him an entire generation older than the United States!

In the early 1990s, India tried to solve its problem of corpses in the Ganges River by releasing 25,000 flesh-eating turtles into the river, spending $32 million on the unsuccessful endeavor.

Box turtles can be dangerous to eat—at times they consume poisonous mushrooms and the toxins may linger in their flesh.

Desert-dwelling toadhead agama lizards communicate by curling and uncurling their tails.

VITAL BUSINESS

FACINATING FACTS
A Snappy Sting

Snapping turtles have a powerful beak-like jaw that really packs a punch! They are known for being fierce and grumpy, particularly when out of water. Unlike other turtles, they can't hide fully inside their shells, which is why they have developed a snapping defense.

MALAGASY LEAF-NOSED SNAKE

As their name implies, leaf-nosed snakes have bizarre nasal appendages. These snakes are often seen hanging from branches with their heads pointing toward the ground, although researchers have not figured out why.

GECKO VISION

A SIGHT FOR SORE EYES

Gecko eyes don't just come in various colors and sizes, they are also incredibly powerful. They can see in the dark, and their night vision is so acute they can even see various shades of color!

Just like snakes, most geckos don't have eyelids, but instead have clear scales over their eyes that they actually lick with their tongues to keep clean. Geckos can also focus sharply on objects at two different depths at the same time. These amazing eyes are colorful and impressive indeed.

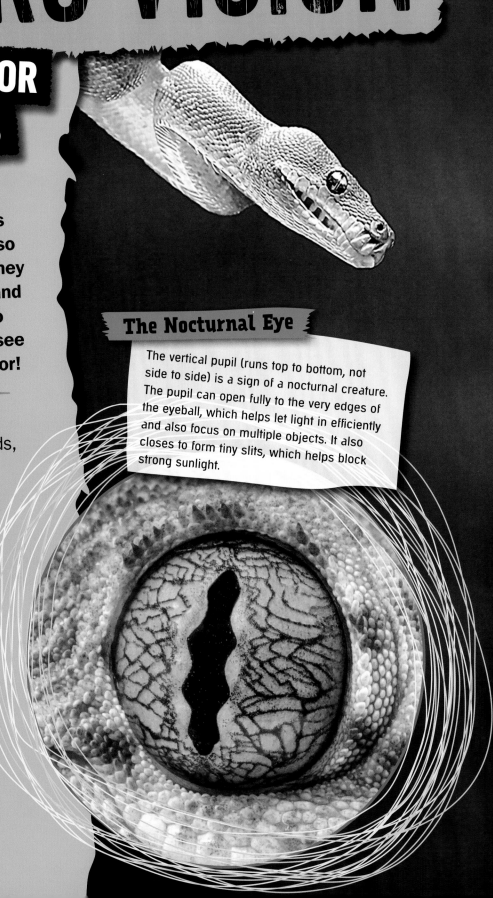

The Nocturnal Eye

The vertical pupil (runs top to bottom, not side to side) is a sign of a nocturnal creature. The pupil can open fully to the very edges of the eyeball, which helps let light in efficiently and also focus on multiple objects. It also closes to form tiny slits, which helps block strong sunlight.

FIELD OF VISION

Geckos, like other reptiles, even shed their eye scales (called spectacles), and their eyes might temporarily look milky or grey/blue during this process.

With eyesight comparable to a cat's, geckos can see better than any other lizard whose vision has been studied.

The sensitivity of most gecko eyes to light is estimated to be about 350 times stronger than human eyes!

In parts of Southeast Asia, tokay geckos are regarded as harbingers of luck and good fortune!

The name gecko comes from the Indonesian Malay language's *gekoq*, which isn't actually a real word but an imitation of the sound geckos make.

Madagascar Velvet Gecko

The Madagascar velvet gecko—including its eyes—is patterned to blend with logs and rocks.

BIG WORD ALERT

NOCTURNAL

Awake and active at night and asleep during the day.

SAVVY SQUEEZERS!

SNAKES THAT LEAVE YOU BREATHLESS

This class of snakes includes pythons, boas, and the giant anaconda. Before swallowing their prey whole, constrictor snakes wrap around their prey and use their extremely strong muscles to squeeze them to death.

When the unfortunate victim breathes out, the snake coils even more tightly so it can't breathe in again. These long, heavy-bodied snakes are built to handle digesting a gigantic meal over several days or even weeks.

Boa constrictor

Snakes like this boa constrictor ambush their prey, using their teeth to grab and force the meal down its throat. While digesting a meal, the snake is vulnerable because it can't move or defend itself easily.

Anacondas can grow to between 25 and 30 feet and weigh over 550 pounds.

Giant anaconda

Anacondas, the largest of the constrictors, can easily kill and eat something as large as an antelope. After a meal that big, they often go into hiding while the super-sized meal is digested.

True or false?

	TRUE	FALSE
A constrictor snake can swallow prey much bigger than its own head.	✓	☐
Snakes can't breathe while they are swallowing prey.	☐	✓
Some constrictors can weigh over 400 pounds.	✓	☐
Anacondas can go months between meals.	✓	☐
Constrictor snakes can "unhinge" their jaws to swallow giant meals.	☐	✓

Python X-ray

Using a special scanning technique, scientists from Denmark took X-rays of a python digesting a rat. After being swallowed by the snake, the rat gradually disappeared during the course of 132 hours—five and a half days!

Rat

MORTAL COMBAT

REPTILES THAT KILL

Certain reptiles can pose a real threat to humans—but only when humans first threaten their space or safety.

Even the most venomous snakes, hazardous lizards, and aggressive crocodiles have an important place in the ecosystem. Remember, these animals might seem like they are out to get you, but like all living things, they are just trying to survive.

Taipan

The taipan, found in Asia and Australia, is a large, fast-moving snake. Its venom is very toxic, and it's considered one of the deadliest known snakes in the world. Luckily, it doesn't live near humans, so bites are rare.

Saw-scaled viper

This highly venomous snake is found in Africa and the Middle East, and it takes the title of deadliest snake because of its nasty, aggressive temper—it often strikes at anything that disturbs it. Interestingly, it is also known for the "sizzling" warning sound it makes before it bites down on its victims.

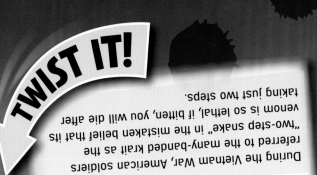

During the Vietnam War, American soldiers referred to the many-banded krait as the "two-step snake." in the mistaken belief that its venom is so lethal, if bitten, you will die after taking just two steps.

In March 2014, wildlife officials finally apprehended a young Nile crocodile in Florida's Everglades National Park. The juvenile croc had escaped from a Miami-Dade facility and was on the run for two years!

Hefty, aggressive monsters, Nile crocodiles kill up to 200 people every year.

The puff adder's venom can kill a human in about 30 minutes. In 2009, a 23-year-old British woman was bit by a puff adder while hiking in Africa and survived without antivenom after more than two hours en route to the hospital.

FIERCE FOES

Green iguana

These iguanas might look friendly, but if they become agitated, they will bite down with their razor-sharp teeth or use their tail as a powerful, painful whip. It's not a good idea to keep these guys as pets!

Gaboon viper

This venomous viper is found in the rainforests and woodlands of Africa. Generally unaggressive and tolerant, these snakes have the longest fangs and deliver the biggest dose of venom of any snake.

Ripley's Believe It or Not!®

While walking around Australia in a *Star Wars* stormtrooper costume to raise money for Monash Children's Hospital, Scott Loxley was attacked by a deadly King Brown snake. The snake tried to bite Loxley on his shin—but was stopped by the plastic costume!

Gila monster

The Gila monster (pronounced HEE-lah) is the largest lizard native to the southwestern United States and northern Mexico—and one of the world's only venomous lizards. A Gila monster will latch on to a victim and chew, allowing neurotoxins to move through the venom glands in its lower jaw and into the open wound.

REPTILES AT RISK

HOW CAN WE SAVE THEM?

Critically Endangered Turtles

The critically endangered list includes several turtles, like the hawksbill sea turtle and the leatherback sea turtle. Many conservation groups help save turtles by encouraging fishermen to use different hooks and nets that don't ensnare turtles, passing laws that make it illegal to sell turtle eggs, and creating safe nesting sites where turtle eggs are protected from humans and other predators.

Every year, more than 250,000 sea turtles are accidentally caught in fishing nets and then drown because they can't get to the surface to breathe.

More fisherman are moving to "turtle excluder devices," which have trap doors that allow smaller trapped turtles to escape, but they don't work as well with large species like the leatherback.

This safe hatchery created by conservationists in Costa Rica protects the leatherback sea turtle eggs from poachers and other predators. Their efforts are working because the number of female turtles returning each year to lay eggs is slowly rising.

Whether it's habitat destruction and pollution, over-hunting and overfishing, or environmental changes, many reptiles are now on the endangered list, meaning they are in danger of becoming extinct.

Although there are natural changes to a reptile's habitat that can endanger it, man-made problems—like poaching—cause the most damage and increase the risk of extinction. We need to make changes before they are gone forever!

More than one-third of all reptile species are threatened, which means they could be endangered in the near future unless they are fully protected.

Many types of Crocodilians are endangered, like this Chinese alligator. Their homes are being turned into rice paddies, and farmers consider them pests and kill them. They are also being eaten as part of traditional Chinese medicine.

BIG WORD ALERT
POACHING
The illegal hunting, killing, or capturing of wild animals.

Many lizards and tortoises are at risk due to loss of habitat, poaching, and the active wildlife trade, especially the critically endangered day gecko and the beautiful radiated tortoise.

What You Can Do

Visit your local zoo or animal sanctuary to learn more about the reptiles in your area. You can also visit websites such as the Sea Turtle Conservancy (www.conserveturtles.org) to find out what you can do to help turtles in danger. Finally, don't buy any reptile products unless you know they come from a legal supplier.

INDEX

Bold numbers refer to main entries; numbers in *italic* refer to illustrations

ACKNOWLEDGMENTS

COVER (sp) Kevin Horan/Getty Images, (b/l) © Nick Garbutt/naturepl.com; **2** (t) © Dennis van de Water - Shutterstock.com; **3** (t) Dave Beaudette, (b/r) © EcoView/Fotolia.com; **4** (sp) Kevin Horan/Getty Images; **6** (t/r) Jason Edwards/National Geographic Creative; **6–7** (dp) © Daniel Heuclin/naturepl.com, (bgd) Mattias Klum/National Geographic Creative; **7** (b) Andy Rouse/Getty Images; **8** (b/l) © JanelleLugge/iStock.com, (b/r) © EuroPics[CEN]; **8–9** (dp) © Elliotte Rusty Harold/Shutterstock.com; **9** (t/c) © Edwin Giesbers/naturepl.com, (b) © Daniel Heuclin/naturepl.com, (b/r) © Teerapun/Shutterstock.com; **10** (l) © EcoView/Fotolia.com, (c/r) Geoeye Satellite Image; **10–11** (dp) © Jurgen Freund/naturepl.com; **11** (t) © hadkhanong/Fotolia.com, (r) Piotr Naskrecki/Minden Pictures/National Geographic Creative; **12** (b) © Cathy Keifer/Fotolia.com; **12–13** (dp) © mgkuijpers/Fotolia.com; **13** (t) © LightRecords/Shutterstock.com, (b) © James DeBoer/Shutterstock.com; **14** (b/r) Seers Croft Vet Surgery; **14–15** (dp) © Stephen Dalton/naturepl.com; **15** (b/l) Linda Davidson / The Washington Post via Getty Images, (b/r) Rob Brookes / Barcroft Media; **16–17** (dp) Mauricio Handler/National Geographic Creative; **17** (t) © Anup Shah/naturepl.com, (b/r) © Pete Oxford/naturepl.com, (c/l) State Archives of Florida, Florida Memory, http://floridamemory.com/items/show/82911; **18** (b/l) © reptiles4all/Shutterstock.com, (b/r) Joel Sartore/National Geographic Creative; **18–19** (dp) © Stuart G Porter - Shutterstock.com; **19** (t/l) Joel Sartore/National Geographic Creative, (t/r) © amwu/iStock.com, (b/l) Dave Beaudette; **20** (b/l) © Anup Shah/naturepl.com, (t/r) R. D. Bartlett; **20–21** (dp) © Daniel Heuclin/naturepl.com; **22** (t) © Sprocky/Shutterstock.com; **22–23** (dp) © Alex Mustard/naturepl.com; **23** (c/r) © Millard H. Sharp / Science Source, (b) © Stephen Dalton/naturepl.com; **24** (b) © Andrea Izzotti/Fotolia.com; **24–25** (dp) Jim Abernethy/National Geographic Creative; **25** (t/l) © atosan/iStock.com, (t/r) © Kitch Bain/Shutterstock.com; **26** (b/r) Jason Edwards/National Geographic Creative; **26–27** (dp) © Doug Perrine/naturepl.com; **27** (b/r) © Pete Oxford/naturepl.com; **28** (t/r) © Renphoto/iStock.com, (b/l) HEIDI AND HANS-JURGEN KOCH/ MINDEN PICTURES/National Geographic Creative; **29** (sp) © Michael D. Kern/naturepl.com, (t/l) Simon D. Pollard / Science Source, (t/r) Courtesy of Sunshine Serpents; **30** (b/r) © Ethan Daniels/Shutterstock.com; **30–31** (dp) © Peter B. Kaplan / Science Source; **31** (t/r) Carnegie Mellon University/Rex/REX USA, (b/l) © Tim MacMillan / John Downer Pr/naturepl.com; **32** (t/r) © Bernard Castelein/naturepl.com, (b/l) © Dimitris Poursanidis / terrasolutions / www.terrasolutions.eu,MY/naturepl.com; **32–33** (dp) © Bence Mate/naturepl.com; **33** (t/r) © Tim MacMillan /John Downer Pro/naturepl.com, (b/r) ADITYA PERMANA / MERCURY PRESS / CATERS NEWS; **34** (c/l) © Jamie Robertson/naturepl.com, (b) © Eric Gevaert - Shutterstock.com; **34–35** (c) © Pedro Narra/naturepl.com, © albund - Shutterstock.com; **35** (t/r) Frans Lanting / MINT IMAGES / Science Source, (c/l) Jason Edwards/National Geographic Creative, (c/r) Joel Sartore/National Geographic Creative; **36** (c/r) Steve Cooper / Science Source, (b/l) © Rosa Jay - Shutterstock.com; **36–37** (bgd) © juan sanchez - Shutterstock.com; **37** (t) Omid Mozaffari, (c) © Michiel de Wit - Shutterstock.com, (b/r) © Dennis van de Water - Shutterstock.com; **38** (b) © reptiles4all - Shutterstock.com; **38–39** (dp) MANG DAY / MERCURY PRESS / CATERS NEWS; **39** (r) Thomas Marent/ MINDEN PICTURES/National Geographic Creative; **40** (b) © Christophe Courteau/naturepl.com; **40–41** (dp) © Nick Garbutt/naturepl.com; **41** (r) Henrik Lauridsen, Kasper Hansen, Michael Pederson, and Tobias Wang; **42** (t) © reptiles4all - Shutterstock.com, (b) © Tony Phelps/naturepl.com; **42–43** (bgd) © DVARG - Shutterstock.com; **43** (t/r) © John Cancalosi/naturepl.com, (c/l) Philip Blackman/Monash Health, (c/r) Joel Sartore/National Geographic Creative, (b/r) © reptiles4all/iStock.com; **44** (c) © Jordi Chias/naturepl.com, (b/l) Jason Edwards/National Geographic Creative, (b/r) © italiansight/iStock.com; **44–45** (bgd) © rangizzz - Shutterstock.com, © Picsfive - Shutterstock.com, © PeterPhoto123 - Shutterstock.com; **45** (t/l) Brian J. Skerry/National Geographic Creative, (t/r) © Laures/iStock.com, (c) © Ryan M. Bolton - Shutterstock.com, (b) © hakoar/iStock.com

Key: t = top, b = bottom, c = center, l = left, r = right, sp = single page, dp = double page, bgd = background

All other photos and artwork are from Ripley's Entertainment Inc.

Every attempt has been made to acknowledge correctly and contact copyright holders and we apologize in advance for any unintentional errors or omissions, which will be corrected in future editions.